Berry, James R.

Medicines from the sea

DATE			
OCT	P-3	W4	JAN 1
[illegible]	S	W-4	JAN 14
NOV 13	S	P-4	MAR 8
FEB 6	S-3	P-3	MAY 1
MAY	E-2	W-4	SEP 6
5	P-3	W-4	OCT 5
JAN 10	W	D-3	SEP 4
MAR 20	-4	M-3	
MAY 16	V-2	F+H	
JAN 20	P-3	LB-2	MAY 10
FEB 20	C-2	VM-2	MAR 28
Flowers			

Medicines from the Sea

Medicines from the Sea

James R. Berry

A W. W. NORTON BOOK
Published by
GROSSET & DUNLAP, INC.
A National General Company
New York

To Noemi, Stephanie, and Ronan

Library of Congress Catalog Card Number: 79-182008
ISBN: 0-448-21427-X (trade edition)
ISBN: 0-448-26197-9 (library edition)
Published Simultaneously in Canada

Printed in the United States of America

The author and publisher wish to thank the following sources for allowing us to use their photographs:

Biological Sciences Curriculum Study: 6, 81
Lederle Laboratories: 7, 33
H. W. Kitchen from National Audubon Society: 20 top
Ron Curbow from National Audubon Society: 30
Hal. H. Harrison from National Audubon Society: 51
Arthur Ambler from National Audubon Society: 61
Robert Hermes from National Audubon Society: 83
Ward's Natural Science Establishment, Inc.: 20 bottom, 78
Westinghouse: 40
American Museum of Natural History: 56, 70
Wide World Photos: 66

Contents

CHAPTER ONE

Nursery of Life

Finally it rained.

The first drops spattered onto the hot rock and hissed into steam. More drops followed and soon a river of water flowed from the sky. In the beginning, clouds of thick steam billowed into the atmosphere. But later, much later, the water trickled off and collected in small pools and lakes.

During this time, sheets of lightning steadily streaked from clouds above toward the rock below. Flashes from these lightning strokes momentarily brightened the thickly overcast and gloomy day. Thunder continuously boomed through the atmosphere, muffled by the dense sheets of rain pouring from the heavens. The pools and lakes of collected water overflowed, joined, and ran downhill in rivers, emptying into giant, bowllike depressions in the earth.

The formation of the seas was underway.

No one can say exactly when these rains began. But scientists have analyzed today's rock formations, measured radioactive decay of certain elements, and studied the atmosphere of earth and other planets. From these and other findings they have pinpointed the sequence of events, and their approximate time, leading to the sea's beginnings.

Everyone agrees that at first the earth was a hot, fiery ball circling the sun. This ball of molten rock and hot gases formed about five billion years ago. As the earth slowly cooled, its crust shifted and contracted, squeezing up mountains from its surface, leaving large valleys and basins. Volcanoes erupted and spewed gases and water vapor trapped inside the earth into the atmosphere.

This water vapor rose, expanded, and cooled. At some point enough water vapor collected high in the atmosphere to form raindrops. Then the rains began.

At first, the rain simply turned into steam, carrying off heat and helping to cool the roasting rock that was earth. Then, at first only in a few scattered places, the earth cooled below the boiling point of water. Here, the rain, instead of bursting into steam, formed hot pools. Eventually, several billion years or so after its formation, the entire earth cooled to below water's boiling point. Now, all the rain flowed to the giant basins that were to become the seas.

The rain continued for perhaps one billion years.

The black, heavy clouds grew thinner as the water inside them fell to earth. Then, one historic day, a patch of clear sky showed through. A ray of sun beamed toward earth, the first streak of sunlight to reach its surface in several eons.

Perhaps it took many more millions of years—no one can say for sure—before most of the clouds had wrung themselves out. But finally they did and huge patches of sunlight streamed to the ground. This light fell on a barren, rocky planet covered with large areas of water—the seas.

Plants were the first living things to form. The rains had washed calcium, salt, sulphur, phosphorus, and other minerals found on land into the waters. The seas absorbed other chemicals such as carbon dioxide from the air. Somehow, over more eons of time, single living cells made from these and other minerals formed and reproduced. The earth's atmosphere at first contained no oxygen. So, these single cells had to do without it.

Some of these cells probably lived on minerals, just as some of today's bacteria use iron, petroleum, and sulphur as their principal food. But eventually, these cells manufactured a vital chemical called chlorophyll, which gives the plant its green color. Thanks to this substance, they were able to use the energy of sunlight plus the carbon dioxide in the sea to live on. These organisms, just as the plants of today, breathed out a waste product: oxygen.

Over further millions of years other organisms evolved that ate plant life, and each other, for food. They also absorbed the oxygen that was not dissolved in seawater to metabolize their dinners. These organisms were the first animals.

The first plants and animals were simply built, mostly of just one cell. Gradually, through the slow steady change of evolution, they became more complex. Sponges appeared on the shallow bottoms of the seas, near land. Jellyfish—the first organisms to have a mouth and stomach—floated on the vast oceans like castaway blobs of protoplasm. Sea worms, the first animals with a brain and nervous system, crawled over the sea's bottom, scavenging for food. Then came lobsters, starfish, and other animals with protective shells. Finally fish, the first animals with backbones—and our ancestors—evolved.

Plants, too, changed. From the microscopic algae came the many kinds of seaweed that flourish in the oceans. But ocean plants never gave rise to the incredible number of species that animal life produced. In fact, most marine plants remain close to the primitive state they were in millions of years ago. It was when plants began to grow on land that they assumed the many varieties we see today.

Today, five billion or so years later, the ocean covers about 70 percent of the earth's surface. Its average depth is over two miles. Each cubic mile of seawater holds a calculated 200 million tons of chemicals: over 6 million tons of magnesium, 500 tons of rubidium, 45 tons of molybdenum, 38 pounds of gold, and quantities of dozens of other elements.

And, these seas swarm with roughly 500,000 different species, or kinds, of marine animals—some so outlandish they could have been spawned on other planets. So many different kinds of animals, and so many of each kind, live in the sea that they total about four-fifths, 80 percent, of *all* animal life on earth.

Plants grow in enormous quantities, too. An estimated 4,000 *tons* of plant life, on average, live in each square mile of sea. So much vegetation grows in the oceans—far more than on land—that most of the earth's oxygen is released by marine, not land plants.

The sea, and its resources, have become the focus of many scientific specialties. In some countries, the oceans are farmed for their food, with huge bays sealed off where fish are raised then harvested periodically. Huge, specially constructed ships suck up magnesium nodules and diamonds from the ocean floor like giant undersea vacuum cleaners. Special submarines can descend to many ocean floors to search out and catalog mineral resources on the oceans' bottom.

Yet one other specialty that views the seas with mounting excitement is marine pharmacology, the science of finding medicines from marine plants and animals. Experts in this field view marine life as a fantastic treasure chest of therapeutic substances. These potential drugs include everything derived from land sources—from aspirin to insulin, anticoagulants to antibiotics. In fact, specialists in this field claim that the sea is a vastly superior source of drugs and medicines, some that will undoubtedly accomplish therapeutic feats so far undreamed of. Let's see why.

Since the seas were the nursery of life, marine animals and plants have had millions of years more than land organisms to evolve. They've grown into an incredible variety of life forms—thousands more than found on land. And, each kind of life form produces enzymes, hormones, toxins, and other substances —collectively they're known as biochemicals—

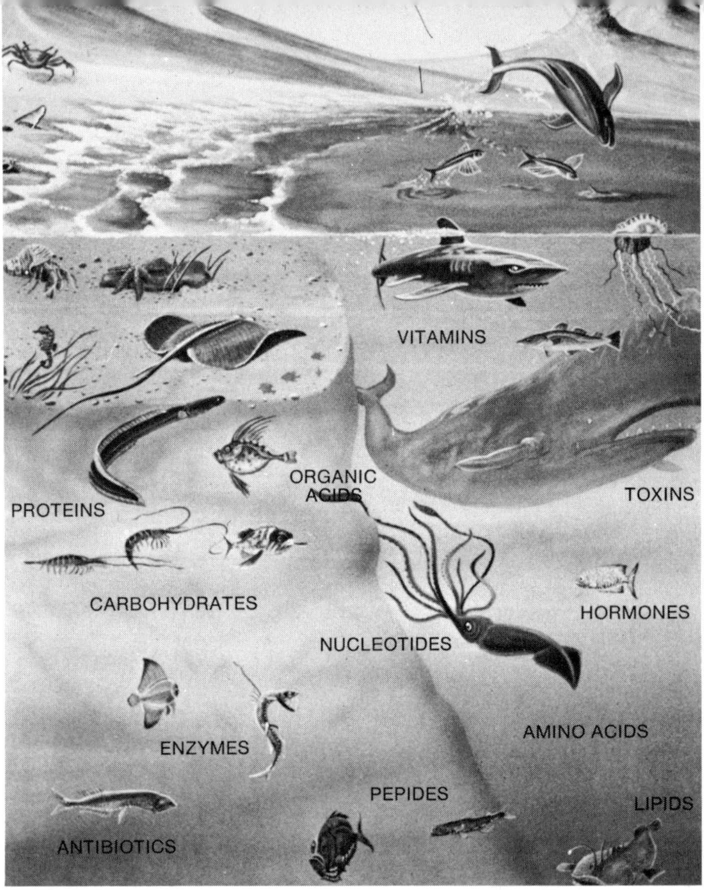

The sea holds a wealth of living creatures and organic substances, any of which may yield a new life-saving drug.

peculiar to it and it alone. Since there are many more kinds of marine organisms than on land, there are hundreds more of these biochemicals, any one of which could turn out to be a helpful drug.

The job of the marine pharmacologist is to discover new biochemicals and see if they can be put to work for mankind.

There's no doubt at all that the sea produces therapeutic biochemicals. This has been known throughout history. The Chinese used various kinds of seaweeds to treat throat diseases. They also used poisons found in certain fish to aid an affliction called sciatica, severe pain caused by

The first step in turning sea life into useful drugs is collecting samples of a plant or animal for study. Here two marine researchers scoop up sea life on the ocean floor.

nerves in the thigh. The ancient Romans used ground up sting ray barbs for treatment of toothaches. And, in the South Sea islands, natives still preserve and store fish by wrapping them in certain kinds of seaweeds.

Superstition?

Today, scientists know that seaweeds have a high iodine content, which aids throat goiter, a common throat disease of people living in mountain areas. The Chinese probably didn't know that iodine cured this malady, but they realized that seaweed helped. In addition, researchers now know that some seaweeds contain antibiotic substances which do delay spoiling of fish.

Further, marine scientists have found that some fish poisons, in small doses, are pain killers and could well dull the agony of sciatica. And, while ground up sting ray barbs aren't found on drugstore shelves today, chances are they did help many a Roman survive a bad toothache—even though no one as yet has looked into the reasons for their possible effect.

But, while folkloric remedies from the sea aren't recent news, scientific sifting of marine organisms for medicines has just really begun. "So far we've studied about one percent of all the sea organisms we *know* contain biologically active material," says Dr. Bruce Halstead, among the country's best known bio-marine authorities. "Compared to other sciences marine pharmacology is at the age of Pasteur."

But the field is picking up headway. Government organizations, foundations, research institutes, and individual scientists are focusing more and more attention on marine organisms and the potential therapeutic agents they contain. As a result, more research teams than ever before are zeroing in on the mysteries of marine life, painstakingly uncovering how a marine plant or animal, or a substance it produces, ticks.

The following chapters discuss just how these men go about their work—and the sea creatures and plants that are the targets of their interest.

CHAPTER TWO

Case of the Beating Heart

It can be found slowly squirming across the ocean floors in waters 60 to 3,000 feet deep and over. It's about 12 inches long, and if you saw one in murky waters it would resemble a slithering eel. Its food is dead or dying fish, and when it spots a meal it bites onto it with a powerful mouth. Its tongue, lined with rows of sharp, rasplike teeth saw through the prey's skin. The animal then eats the insides of the fish, leaving only a bag of skin and bones that floats to the sea's floor like a deflated balloon.

This marine animal is the hagfish. And, it produces a biochemical that might someday help thousands of people weakened by heart disease.

The hagfish is a primitive sea animal with no jaw or stomach—only a single intestine stretching from one end of the animal to the other. It breathes in seawater through one nostril, the only one it has. Not two, but twelve pairs of gills—six pairs in some species—extract oxygen from this water. Like many other animals that

The hagfish cleans its defensive slime from its body by squeezing itself through its own knot.

inhabit the floor of the oceans, it has no real eyes. In their place are two whitish spots that are sensitive to light. The hagfish can tell the difference between light and dark, but no more.

Compensating for its blindness, the hagfish has a remarkable sense of smell and touch. Three pairs of stubby tentacles about a quarter of an inch long serve as sensors. When the hagfish feels hunger, it swims slowly through the waters, its head turning gently from side to side against the small ocean currents that exist even on the sea's floor. Its fleshy sensors stand out, alert for the scent of a weak or dead fish. Once it spots a possible meal, the slow-moving hagfish becomes a frantic mass of squirming flesh. It strikes at its prey, burrows through its skin, and gulps down its meal quickly and efficiently.

Hagfish have no known enemies, probably because of one of the most unusual defense mechanisms nature has invented. If attacked or even annoyed, the hagfish secretes a thick slime from glands along its body. On contact with water, this slime expands into a protective, sticky shield that entangles an enemy. Once the danger is over, the hagfish cleans this goo from its body by tying itself in a knot. Through some sort of muscular judo, the hagfish moves through its own knot, the loop descending toward its tail and wiping away the slime as it does so. If some muck gets in the hagfish's nostril, it blows it out with a short, powerful sneeze.

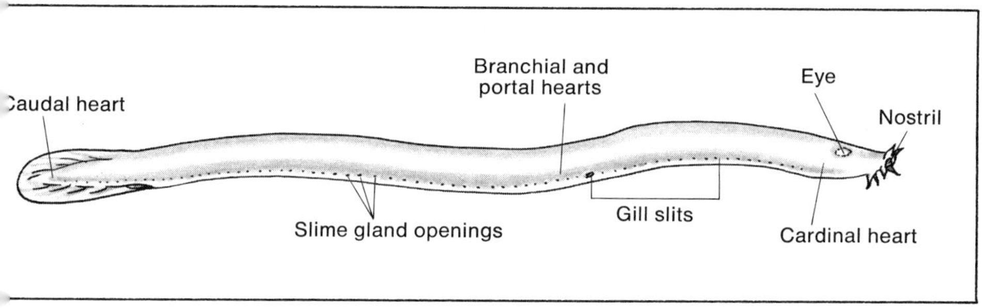

The hagfish has four distinct hearts, each one independent of the other. One of its hearts is located in its tail.

Besides having slime as a protection, a tongue lined with teeth, no jaws or stomach, the hagfish sports an even stranger characteristic: four hearts, each totally independent of one another.

Hagfish hearts aren't regulated by nerves, as are hearts in man and most other animals, and for a simple reason. This marine animal doesn't have a sympathetic nervous system, the network of nerves that governs the heartbeat in mammals. A quirk of evolution explains this combination of four actively beating hearts and no nervous system to regulate them.

At one time, life forms in the sea hadn't evolved to the point of developing a nervous system. The hagfish belongs to this period. Since it has an effective defense mechanism and an abundant food supply, the hagfish didn't have to evolve into something different to survive. The result is an animal that is almost identical to the hagfishes swimming in the seas millions of years ago.

Naturally, since the hagfish doesn't have a nervous system to control its hearts, other factors keep these organs beating. These other factors are what interested Dr. David Jensen, a physiologist especially interested in the mechanisms that drive hearts. The hagfish offered a unique advantage to his research.

Here's why. The hagfish heart is much like the human heart in embryonic form. After a baby is conceived, its cells begin to multiply rapidly. In a few weeks, this fledgling baby, or embryo, resembles a primitive form of life, looking more like a tadpole than a human being. At this point, its lungs, liver, kidneys, brain, and other organs are merely clumps of cells. Only as the embryo grows older do these cells develop into specific body units.

Curiously, before an organ becomes fully

grown, it passes through stages where it resembles the same organ of a primitive animal.

The heart is no exception. At some point in an embryo's life, the muscular wall of its heart begins to twitch irregularly, then pulsate, and finally contract in a steady, rhythmic beat. This steady contraction starts *before* the embryo's nervous system has grown enough to regulate this beat, just like the hagfish heart.

What is the origin of this nerveless heartbeat? Dr. Jensen turned to the hagfish to find out.

Luckily, the largest of the hagfish's four hearts is about the size of a pea, large enough to dissect and study. So, using this heart, Dr. Jensen began to study what makes it tick.

To test the rate at which the hagfish heart persists in beating, Dr. Jensen carried out some startling experiments. In one instance, he carefully removed a hagfish heart with a scalpel. Then, he planted it under the skin of another hagfish, where it could float in natural body fluids. This transplanted heart kept beating for three weeks inside its new owner. Other implanted hagfish hearts kept up their steady pulsations even longer.

In another experiment, Dr. Jensen took a beating hagfish heart and placed it in ordinary seawater. This small bit of steadily beating tissue had no nourishment, no body to protect it, and no blood to pump. Yet it, and many others treated the same way, kept up its regular strong beat. Only after several days did the beats slow, weaken, and finally stop altogether.

More surprises were to come. Dr. Jensen cut the largest heart of a hagfish into small pieces.

Then he put these pieces, each about the size of a match head, into a salt solution. Even the fragments of hagfish heart kept up their tireless contractions for days before dying.

Dr. Jensen tried the same test on the other hearts. The results added one more important fact to his collection.

Tests had shown him that each of the four hagfish hearts beats at a different pace. When scraps of a given heart were put in a salt solution, even the pieces of that heart kept up this and only this pace. Whatever it was that regulated the beat of each nerveless heart, also regulated the beat of pieces of that heart.

What did this regulating?

Dr. Jensen had a good idea that a chemical was one important agent that triggered the beats of hagfish hearts. This idea wasn't new. Half a century ago specialists proposed that certain biochemicals keep hearts of some animals beating regularly. But nobody had ever used modern research methods to find out which, if any, biochemicals did this job. Dr. Jensen decided to fill this gap.

The job took him eleven years because Dr. Jensen faced the same problem that confronts scores of other researchers. Any chemicals made by a marine animal, as well as other living things, are usually mixed with hundreds of other chemicals. Any one of these may be the cause of a given biological effect. Some of the biochemicals in ground up hagfish hearts regulated cell growth, metabolism, or any one of many functions important to life. Dr. Jensen knew that probably just one biochemical regulated heartbeats. And his thorniest job was to isolate only that biochemical.

Only a few decades ago the job might not have been possible. Today, researchers have many recently developed or perfected tools that they use to isolate one biochemical from many others. One method, a simple and common procedure, is paper chromatography.

Essentially, a solution containing the various biochemicals is dropped onto the edge of a sheet of absorbent paper. The paper is held vertically by clamps, the solution slowly flowing through the paper from the top edge to the bottom edge. The heaviest biochemicals flow through the paper fastest and reach bottom first. The lightest biochemicals remain near the top. Once the liquid evaporates, the biochemicals—each a different weight and usually of a slightly different color—are separated as streaks on the paper. Then these streaks are tested one by one to see which is responsible for a given effect.

A variation of this technique is ascending chromatography, where the edge of the paper is held in a solution. Capillary action draws the liquid up, which, as it evaporates, leaves its composite biochemicals at different heights.

Using this latter method, as well as more specialized procedures, Dr. Jensen finally found the biochemical that would cause hearts of live hagfish to flutter. He called this white crystalline substance that resembles sugar grains, eptatretin. And, it turned out to be among the most powerful heart regulators known to man.

In one experiment, Dr. Jensen placed some frog hearts, which remain alive for an hour or so after being taken from their hosts, in a salt solution. The hearts pumped away at 30 beats a minute. Then he added a minute speck of eptatretin. The pace of the beats began to pick up, and within two minutes reached 40 pulses every 60 seconds. They kept up this quick rate as long as eptatretin was in the solution.

In another instance, Dr. Jensen injected eptatretin into the veins of several healthy dogs. Their pulse quickened, blood pressure rose, and heartbeat strengthened. This proved to him that the drug works on animals closely related to man.

One of the most significant experiments came when Dr. Jensen deliberately caused the equivalent of a heart attack in a dog and injected eptatretin into its veins. Almost immediately, the biochemical jolted the animal's heart back to life. From a weak, irregularly pulsing organ, the dog's heart became a strong mass of muscle with a steadily defined beat. Dr. Jensen tried the same experiment on dozens of other animals. The results were the same.

And eptatretin's use for man?

Eptatretin might someday be used as a drug that regulates the rate of heartbeat in people with damaged heart nerves, or as a new treatment for victims of heart attacks. But there's a long, rocky road from a drug's discovery to its clinical use. It must be tested on thousands of animals, then cautiously on humans. Researchers must note any toxic side effects, then evaluate the drug's overall worth. This process is long and tedious, and so far eptatretin hasn't been used to treat humans.

But it has proven itself a strong potential as a drug that will counter the country's major killer: heart disease. So, thanks to the hagfish, the time may be in sight when a drug that regulates a once dying or weakened heart is in common use.

CHAPTER THREE

Communes of the Sea

They quietly sit there on the ocean floors, often in a rainbow of brilliant colors, ranging in size from a marble to a kitchen stove. These are the sponges, animals dating back far into prehistoric time. Yet somehow, primitive as they are, sponges manufacture complex biochemicals that seem destined to be among the most potent antibiotics, or germ-fighting drugs, known.

Sponges are such an elementary form of life that scientists had a hard time deciding if they are plants or animals. They don't move from one spot to another, as most animals do, to hunt food. Yet, they don't use sunlight to manufacture protein, like plants. Today, sponges are just barely considered animals.

They have no stomach, heart, lungs, brain, or other organs. They are simply masses of single cells which work together toward a common end—keeping alive as a sponge. These cells can live separate from the others. But, over millions of years of evolution, they prefer to live in communes. If a sponge is strained through a fine mesh cloth the cells remain alive. But soon they begin to regroup and form the original sponge again—with each cell doing its former job.

No one knows how these cell communes evolved. Perhaps, millions of years ago, single cells floating in the ocean collided, stuck together, and survived better as a team than when drifting alone. Probably some cells did certain jobs better than others, and all began to depend on the specific jobs the collective family of cells carried out. There is no doubt these cell communes have succeeded as a life form. Sponges are among the hardiest and oldest animals on earth.

Scientists estimate that at least 5,000 different kinds of sponges grow on ocean floors. Most sponges prefer to grow on rocky sea bottoms or coral reefs just offshore continents or islands. But many varieties of sponges live in much deeper water, often adapting to muddy sea bottoms. Some kinds actually sprout roots that grow into the soft ocean floor and anchor the animal firmly in place. Even the strongest ocean currents can't wash these sponges away.

Since sponges can't wander from their post and hunt for food, they bring their meals to themselves. Sponges are peppered with thousands of tiny pores that lead to a central cavity inside the animal. Small, microscopically thin tentacles inside these pores whip the water into the cavity. With the water come small, one-celled plants and animals. Specialized cells in the sponge's central cavity digest this nourishment and distribute it to the rest of the

Sponges grow in relatively shallow water near coasts. About 5,000 kinds exist, including the variety above that attaches itself to underwater rocks, and the bottom variety that is large enough to hide the hermit crab on whose shell it lives.

animal. A sponge the size of a basketball might take in five gallons of water a day through its pores. An even larger sponge can gulp in 600 gallons a day.

To support a sponge's weight, cells within the animal build a skeleton that branches out like twigs on a tree limb. Some sponges manufacture this skeleton principally from calcium. Others mainly use silicon, present in seawater, as their skeleton's material—the same substance used to make glass.

There are exceptions to the rule that sponges don't move from their birthplace. At least one kind grows only on empty shells that once belonged to large marine snails. This same kind of shell attracts hermit crabs, which use them as a home. As hermit crabs wander across the ocean floor searching for food, they carry their homes with them, and the sponge on top.

Marine pharmacologists became interested in sponges because of a once puzzling characteristic of these animals. Sponge beds, even those covering thousands of square feet are surprisingly clean.

In any given area of the ocean's bottom, fish and plants die and begin to rot. Yet, when this happens in sponge beds, the water remains pure. Somehow, the decaying dead matter doesn't pollute water around sponges. In fact, sponges even clean up many of man's pollutants. Off the coast of Jamaica, sewage from Kingston, the capital city of this Caribbean island, empties into the ocean. A huge forest of sponges lives offshore. However, the water in this far-flung sponge bed shows no sign of the sewage bacteria, which flourishes where no sponges exist.

Marine researchers suspected that some biochemicals made by sponges prevented decay and sewage germs from growing. The idea seemed logical. Since sponges can't swim to clear water, they must have evolved some means of keeping their immediate environment clean. Manufacturing antibiotics or other purifying biochemicals was the likely method. If so, these substances might be useful as pharmaceuticals. The hunt for these biochemicals, based on a scientific hunch, began.

At first the search got off to a slow start. After examining single cells of sponges under powerful microscopes, scientists found that many bacteria seemed to live there. Still other tests revealed that many kinds of microbes live throughout sponges, in large numbers. Since these bacteria seemed comfortable living in their sponge homes, researchers believed that the antibiotics might come from them, and not from the sponge itself. If so, it would be a case of microbes producing antibiotics that killed other microbes.

To find out, researchers grew colonies of bacteria living in sponges on dishes of agar, a clear, gell-like nutrient most germs thrive on. Then, they grew colonies of other, disease causing bacteria. Soon, both colonies of germs were thriving on the agar, turning the nutrient cloudy. At this point it was time to see if the bacteria found in sponges killed other germs or not.

The test was simple. A researcher simply scooped up a bit of agar teeming with the sponge's bacteria, then spread these germs across colonies of the harmful microbes. If these bacteria died the nutrient would become clear again, a positive sign that the germs living there were dead.

But the agar didn't clear. In fact, the bacteria taken from sponges lived happily with the harmful microbes. The antibiotics and other biochemicals didn't come from microbes in the sponges. They were produced by the sponges themselves. Obviously, the microbes found in sponges were somehow immune to these substances.

Now, researchers concentrated on the sponges themselves. But before they began isolating specific antibiotics, they had a more fundamental task ahead of them: discover which sponges secreted the most powerful and effective antibiotics, the ones that had the most potential to help man. Once a few sponges were singled out, the long, often dreary, process of isolating single biochemicals and testing them on animals could begin.

Research teams throughout the country began to test various kinds of sponges for antibiotic activity. The procedure used at Osborn Laboratories in New York, one of the pioneering marine research laboratories, is a good example of how this research is done.

Marine researchers at Osborn Laboratories grew many kinds of germs on agar or other nutrients. Then, they simply dropped pieces of live sponge onto these colonies. If the agar around the sponge cleared after a day or so, they knew that that type of sponge killed the kind of germ growing in the nutrient.

Many varieties of sponge—the heavenly sponge, fire sponge, bleeding sponge, for example, were deadly to a few kinds of harmful bacteria. Then, came the red beard sponge, a species found off the coast of Long Island. This sponge not only killed many kinds of bacteria, but also acted against some that are particularly harmful to man, including those that cause penicillin-resistant staph infections, tuberculosis, trench mouth, and some hard to cure bladder infections. The antibiotic produced by the red beard, if it could be used for humans, would be particularly valuable. Marine researchers at Osborn decided to concentrate on this species, and try to isolate the antibiotic biochemicals it secretes.

Lab technicians ground up dozens of these sponges at a time, and using paper chromatography and other methods separated many chemicals produced by the sponge. After months of work purifying the biochemicals and testing each one to find the antibiotic among them, they singled out the active substance. They named it ectyonin.

Years of tests on animals are necessary before a drug can be tried on human beings. Ectyonin is still being studied for any possible side effects in animals, and for its effectiveness against many kinds of disease germs. So far it shows great promise as a broad spectrum antibiotic, one that wipes out many disease germs at a time. Soon, it may be ready for clinical testing.

But more drugs from sponges are on the way, too. So far, researchers have tested about 1,000 kinds of sponges for signs of antibiotic activity. And, at least one major drug firm has a large-scale research program designed to filter out useful antibiotics from sponges. They've found that 25 percent of sponges tested kill different kinds of disease microbes, and also inhibit or prevent growth of yeasts and fungus, plant forms that also can be harmful to man.

Particularly encouraging is the fact that each kind of sponge produces its own, specific kind of antibiotic. Since there are over 5,000 kinds of sponges, researchers have, roughly, 5,000 substances with which to experiment. Naturally, these figures are inexact. Some antibiotics are immediately ruled out because of their harmful side effects. Others are so weak they wouldn't be helpful. But, all told, sponges represent one of the largest single potential sources of new pharmaceuticals the oceans have to offer.

In addition, researchers have found that some sponge biochemicals are effective against viruses—living matter responsible for many maladies including the common cold, and thought to be a cause of cancer in humans. These biochemicals would have special importance. Today, despite years of experimentation, there is no effective drug commercially available that is effective against viruses.

Yet, in laboratory tests, extracts from certain sponges slowed and actually retarded growth of viruses, and virus-caused tumors. Scientists don't know yet how these biochemicals accomplish this job. But the fact that they do offers hope that research on sponges may someday produce potent antiviral drugs, as well as many effective against microbes. If so, one of nature's oldest animals will have provided some of man's most needed and welcome drugs.

CHAPTER FOUR

Soup to Drugs — the Sea Cucumber

Sunlight filters through the water to a pale blue and gently illuminates the sea anemones, which gently wave in the slow ocean currents. A large fish wanders through the water, hungry. It sights a sausage-shaped animal wriggling through the ooze of the sea bottom. The fish circles closer, eyeing what it considers its next meal. It darts forward, and nudges the two foot long animal.

In a flash, the animal's muscles give a strong, convulsive contraction. From its mouth, which is surrounded by thick, stubby tentacles, it vomits out its insides, including stomach and a thick, sticky phlegmlike substance. The fish feels the soft entanglement of the slimy mass, senses danger, and darts away.

This fish is lucky. In a few moments smaller fish casually swimming near this creature begin to shudder, their fins stiffen. Soon, the small fish and microscopic animal life within a several foot radius of the now quiet marine animal are dead.

Only many minutes later, after the ocean currents have brought in new water, can marine life safely drift back to the area.

The animal that caused this mayhem is the sea cucumber. And, the poison it vomited out along with its guts has turned out to be almost an entire drug factory in itself.

About 500 varieties of sea cucumbers inhabit the oceans; some as small as three or four inches, others as long as three feet. They live on the ocean floors, burrowing through the mud and sand. The tentacles around their mouth have a keen sense of smell, and shovel food they find, along with the mud and sand, into their mouth. Not every kind of sea cucumber regurgitates its insides when attacked. But those varieties that do, grow back these organs within three to four weeks and begin feeding again.

One of the sea cucumbers' most effective enemies is man. In the Orient, sea cucumber soup, called *trepang*, is considered a delicacy. Somehow, any of the deadly poison remaining in these animals is destroyed by gastric juices and cooking.

But soup isn't the only practical use man has for sea cucumbers. In certain South Sea islands, natives dive for these animals, then squeeze the juices inside them into pools that form on coral reefs. There is enough poison still left in the sea cucumbers, even after they have ejected their insides, to kill edible fish in this water. When the dead fish float to the surface, the natives reap their harvest.

The fact that sea cucumbers produce a poison has been known, at least to these natives, for centuries. But the power of the poison and its subsequent study as a potential drug, came about by accident.

In the late 1940's, Dr. Ross Nigrelli, now of New York's Osborn Laboratories, was studying the ability of the sea cucumber to spew out its insides, then regenerate a new set of stomach organs. While on a trip to Bimini, an island near Florida, he put some sea cucumbers in a large tank. Fresh seawater was pumped into this tank through a hose.

Several other tanks were lined up near the first. To keep water in these other tanks fresh, the overflow from the first tank, which held the sea cucumbers, was piped into the second, and so on. In the last tank, about the fifth down the row, were some tropical fish Dr. Nigrelli was also studying.

But first, he wanted to observe exactly how a sea cucumber throws up its insides, and prodded one with a short stick. The animal contracted and emptied out its interior organs. Then, something else caught Dr. Nigrelli's attention. As he glanced over toward the last tank, he noticed that the tropical fish were swimming wildly. They started to shudder, and then, one by one, they died. Poison from the sea cucumber had killed them.

This accidental observation confirmed the fact that sea cucumbers can emit poison. But what really interested Dr. Nigrelli was the power of this biochemical. By the time the fish died, only a small part of water had overflowed into the second tank. An even smaller portion had overflowed into the third. The amount of poison that finally reached the last tank and killed the fish was incredibly small. Whatever substances this poison was made of, they were extremely toxic.

Whenever researchers find a powerful poison they're immediately interested. "Toxicity indicates that something is very biologically active," explains one marine scientist. "From that point on it's a question of seeing if the substance is useful, taming it, and then finding the correct dosage and concentration. Lots of deadly poisons in correct dosages are important drugs. Curare, for example, is used by South American indians to poison their arrow tips. When purified and given in the right amounts, it's used by doctors to control muscle spasms."

When Dr. Nigrelli returned to New York, among his projects was investigating the powerful biochemical of the sea cucumber. Happily there is no shortage of the substance. The poison is stored in an organ called the Cuvierian tubules. These tubules are removed, dried, and powdered. Then the poison is separated from the other organic matter through common laboratory techniques. The result is an orange colored powder.

Dr. Nigrelli called this toxic substance holothurin, and among many other experiments he tested it on several kinds of bacteria for a possible antibiotic effect. It had none. Holothurin may be deadly to fish, but it's harmless to microbes.

More experiments, however, showed that holothurin has an extraordinary variety of other effects. Even in tiny doses it stopped certain cells from developing. Just 66 parts of holothurin

The sea cucumber vomits out its stomach and other inside organs when threatened. Included in this slimy mass is a deadly poison which is now being studied as a possible anticancer and anticlotting drug, and as a possible new anesthetic.

added to one *million* parts of water prevented several kinds of protozoa—microscopically small, one-celled animals—from growing. It also prevented normal development of eggs taken from the sea urchin. And, it had an effect on plant life, too. In various concentrations, holothurin suppressed development of the fine root hairs of watercress, and killed the tips of onion roots.

The fact that holothurin has a repressive effect on growth was particularly interesting to the research team studying the substance. Cancer is the wild, uncontrolled growth of cells. Might holothurin prevent development of such random multiplication?

Research showed it did. The team injected holothurin into mice infected with cancer, one half a fatal dose every other day for 20 days. Other mice, which also had cancer, didn't receive the biochemical. This group died in about two weeks. Those that received the substance lived out their normal life span.

In still other tests, cells that cause mouth cancer in humans were grown in a flask. After holothurin was added, the growth of these cells was greatly retarded, and often stopped completely. At the correct dosages, holothurin had little or no effect on the growth of healthy cells.

Marine researchers at Osborn Laboratories found still another property of holothurin. They mixed the substance with mouse meal and gave it to a batch of experimental mice. Other mice didn't receive the holothurin-enriched meal. Blood from the mice eating holothurin took many times longer to clot than blood from ordinary mice. Injecting holothurin increased its potency so that even less quantities were necessary to prolong clotting time. From this experiment, and others, holothurin has proved itself a possible anticoagulant drug.

Still another effect might be turned to use as a new anesthetic. When scientists pinpointed the reason holothurin killed fish, they found it affected nerve impulses. Signals to and from the brain pass from one nerve to the next. Where two nerves meet is a junction called the synapse. To get to or from the brain, an impulse has to pass across these junctions freely. The process, in theory, is simple. A signal speeds along a nerve, hits a synapse, and causes chemical changes that, in turn, stimulate the next nerve and so on.

Holothurin blocks signals at these junctions. And, without these thousands of nerve signals passing from brain to muscles, animals soon die.

But what's fatal at one dose can be a cure or a help in another. Anesthetics simply block nerve impulses temporarily. A local anesthetic leaves the patient awake, but kills the sensation of pain in a specific area. A general anesthetic kills pain while putting the patient to sleep.

But all anesthetics have side effects, including alteration of the heart beat and respiration. So, physicians are always searching for new anesthetics that kill pain but have fewer or less pronounced side effects. When tamed, holothurin, because of its powerful effect on the synapse, will be a potential candidate for a new anesthetic.

As a bonus, holothurin seems to act as a shark repellent. No one has yet conducted conclusive

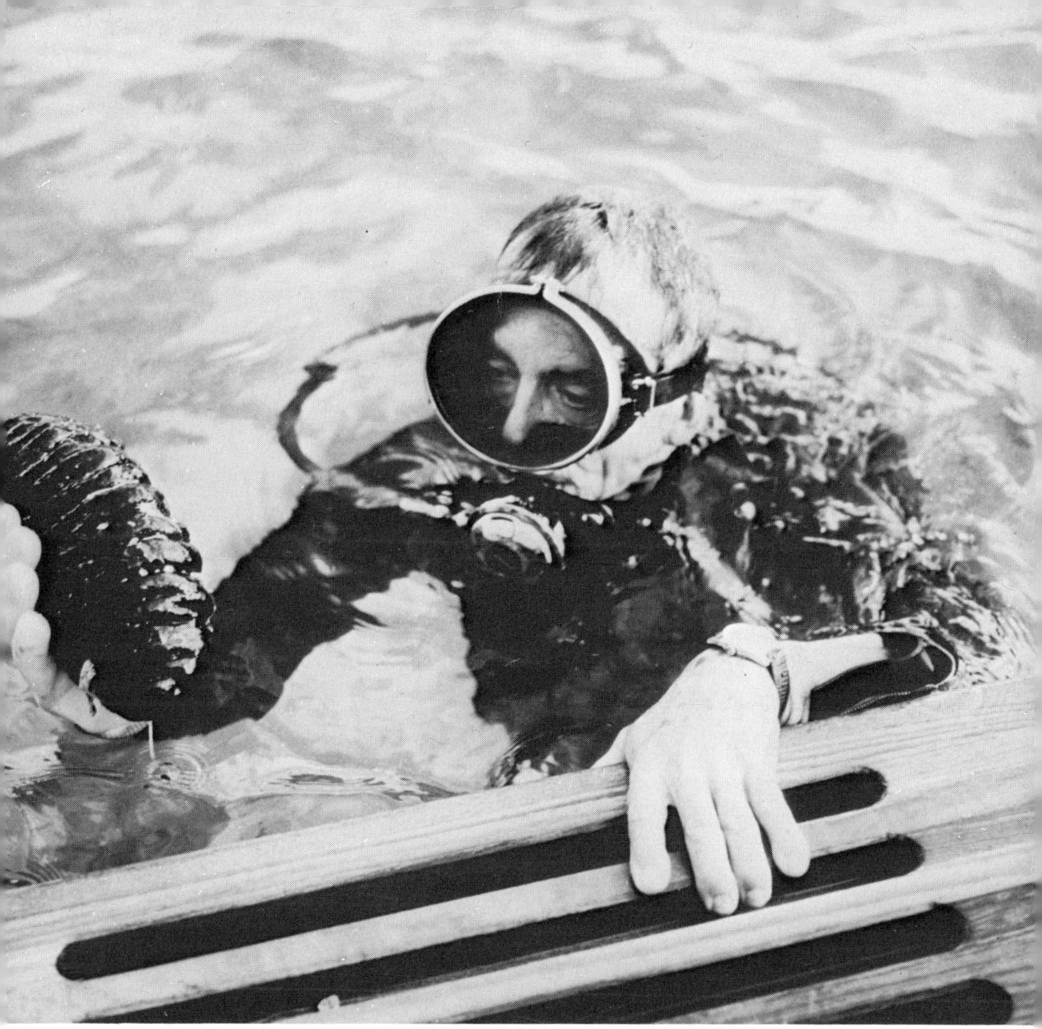

Dr. Paul Burkholder of Lederle Laboratories surfaces with a variety of sea cucumber. This species has shown antifungus activity.

tests with this purpose in view. However, while the poison won't kill an animal as large as a shark when released into water by the sea cucumber, it does seem to warn them away. Only more studies will show if this apparent property is really effective or not.

The biggest problem confronting marine researchers—and the reason holothurin is still such an experimental substance—is its chemical structure.

Holothurin is a complex biochemical, with many different substances latched closely to one another. And, each of these separate substances could become an important drug in itself. Often, a single substance has an important effect, or contributes to an important effect.

Holothurin, for example, has atoms of sulphur in it. With these atoms present, the biochemical blocks nerve transmission. This blocking effect is irreversible, and no antidote can save an animal that is affected by holothurin that includes these sulphur atoms. As an anesthetic, this variety of the biochemical would be fatal.

But, if the sulphur atoms are chemically removed, the blocking effect *is* reversible. Holothurin can be washed off the nerve junction and the signals flow past once again. There is no damage to the synapse. This variety has a potential as a new anesthetic.

The goal of the marine scientist is to remove the parts of the holothurin molecule that cause toxic side reactions, and preserve the part that has the wanted effect. "It's as though you have Siamese triplets," explains a researcher at the Osborn Laboratories. "The different parts of holothurin are locked closely together. They're so closely related and so firmly joined that so far we can't isolate just one without hurting the effect of all."

Consequently, once holothurin is purified, some of its activities are lost. Raw holothurin, for instance, inhibits cancer in mice. The purified product isn't as toxic; it takes a large dose to kill an animal. But it also won't prevent cancer cells from multiplying. Somehow, the active part of the biochemical is lost during the purifying process.

Until each biochemical composing holothurin is identified, and its effects tested, the potential drugs in the substance can't be synthesized. And, until chemists synthesize a drug in their laboratories, it can't be mass produced, and thus isn't really classed as a useful drug.

Right now, researchers are attempting to peg certain parts of the holothurin biochemical with each effect. And, if they do, this poison from the ordinary sea cucumber will stand as another example of how the sea is helping fill man's never-ending need for improved and effective medicines.

CHAPTER FIVE

Eels That Sparked a Discovery

A late morning sun beamed over the cloudless sky of Tijuana, Mexico when the first symptoms began to appear. Doctors throughout the city reported a growing number of similar complaints: headaches, high fevers, severe watering at the mouth, overall weakness, and difficulty breathing. By noon, health officials knew they had a surprise epidemic on their hands.

At first, officials suspected wide-scale food poisoning, a guess that was close to truth, but just enough off the mark to delay treatment for victims of the malady. Then, suspicion shifted to an epidemic of some disease that had suddenly struck the city. By evening both these choices had been ruled out. The symptoms just weren't compatible with any known disease.

More people became ill. By the next day over 1,000 persons had reported that they had the strange fever, chills, headache, and weakness. Hospitals began to fill with serious cases. Then, the first deaths—all of them children—occurred.

Tijuana is too small to have public health laboratories that might have discovered the problem immediately. So, it was on a Sunday—three days after the first cases were reported—that health officers finally found the real cause.

Through questioning many victims, physicians learned that all patients had one thing in common. They had eaten a certain kind of bread before becoming ill. Samples of the bread were sent to a laboratory for analysis. The report handed the town a shock: the bread was poisoned. An insecticide, a deadly variety called parathion, had somehow contaminated it.

Much later an investigation found that cans of parathion had been stored in a warehouse next to bags of sugar. One can had a small hole in it and some of the deadly chemical leaked into bags of sugar. Later, the sugar was used by a local bakery in its bread. This poisoned bread caused the town's epidemic.

Within two days over 600 people were hospitalized. The number of dead children crawled higher, to a final total of 17. But now that doctors had isolated parathion as the poison they knew of a specific antidote. Within hours of injecting this antidote into the victims, all patients recovered. The day this antidote reached Tijuana, the epidemic was over.

These townspeople didn't know it, but the drug that saved further agony and possible deaths was available thanks to the electric eel.

Electric eels aren't eels, they're really a fish—a relative of the catfish family. They are just one of three varieties of fish that generate electricity. But somewhere along their evolution, these fish adapted to fresh water. Today, electric eels can be found only in the Amazon and Orinoco rivers of South America.

Blunt nosed, its eyes blind from cataracts caused by its own constant jolts of electricity, the electric eel easily grows five feet long. Some specimens are even longer. Of the eel's five-foot length, one foot holds the animal's organs. The rest of the creature's length is its electric generator.

These living dynamos can generate a wallop of 600 volts, enough to kill a horse. They also produce low voltage pulses. Electric eels constantly generate a series of 50-volt discharges. Ugly black pits running from the eel's nose down its back somehow pick up reflections from these small jolts. As the eel swims through water, it uses these small discharges, a sort of electrical radar, to avoid obstacles and to sense nearby meals. If these pits are covered the eel becomes helpless. In effect, they are electric ears that replace this fish's eyes.

In the 1930's, biologists found that the electric eel's generator is really a massive quantity of large nerve cells. In fact, it turned out, this animal is made mostly of these cells, which are lined up in neat rows in its tail.

When researchers studied a single cell with electronic instruments, they found it cranked out exactly one-tenth of a volt. Not much by itself, but the electric eel's electricity producing cells are connected in series—the head of one cell linked to the tail of another. And, when hooked up in series, the final voltage is the sum of *all* the cells. Each electric eel cell produces only a fraction of a volt. But added together, these nerves generate a man-killing charge.

Something else caught the attention of specialists interested in the electric eel. This animal's nerve cells look very much like nerves in human beings. Except that they are bigger and more plentiful, given the size of the fish, than in any other animal. The electric eel's nerve cells are so big, in fact, that a single one can be removed and then dissected with the naked eye.

Until World War II, this fact was an interesting observation stored away in scientific journals. Then, military intelligence got wind of some ominous experiments being conducted in Nazi Germany. German scientists, American intelligence learned, were developing powerful nerve gases. If released on allied forces they could paralyze and kill entire armies.

The U.S. Army began its search for an antidote to this new weapon even before it was perfected. Army brass called on Dr. David Nachmansohn, a biochemist specializing in nerve research, to head the project. The army representatives asked if there was any special equipment Dr. Nachmansohn would want. His reply: One hundred electric eels.

It took several months for an order of electric eels, which could only be found in South America, to arrive. But finally, Dr. Nachmansohn received several barrels filled with the squirming and angry animals. With many a shocked shout from laboratory assistants who handled the animals, work on the nerve gas antidote started.

Dr. Nachmansohn began by isolating single

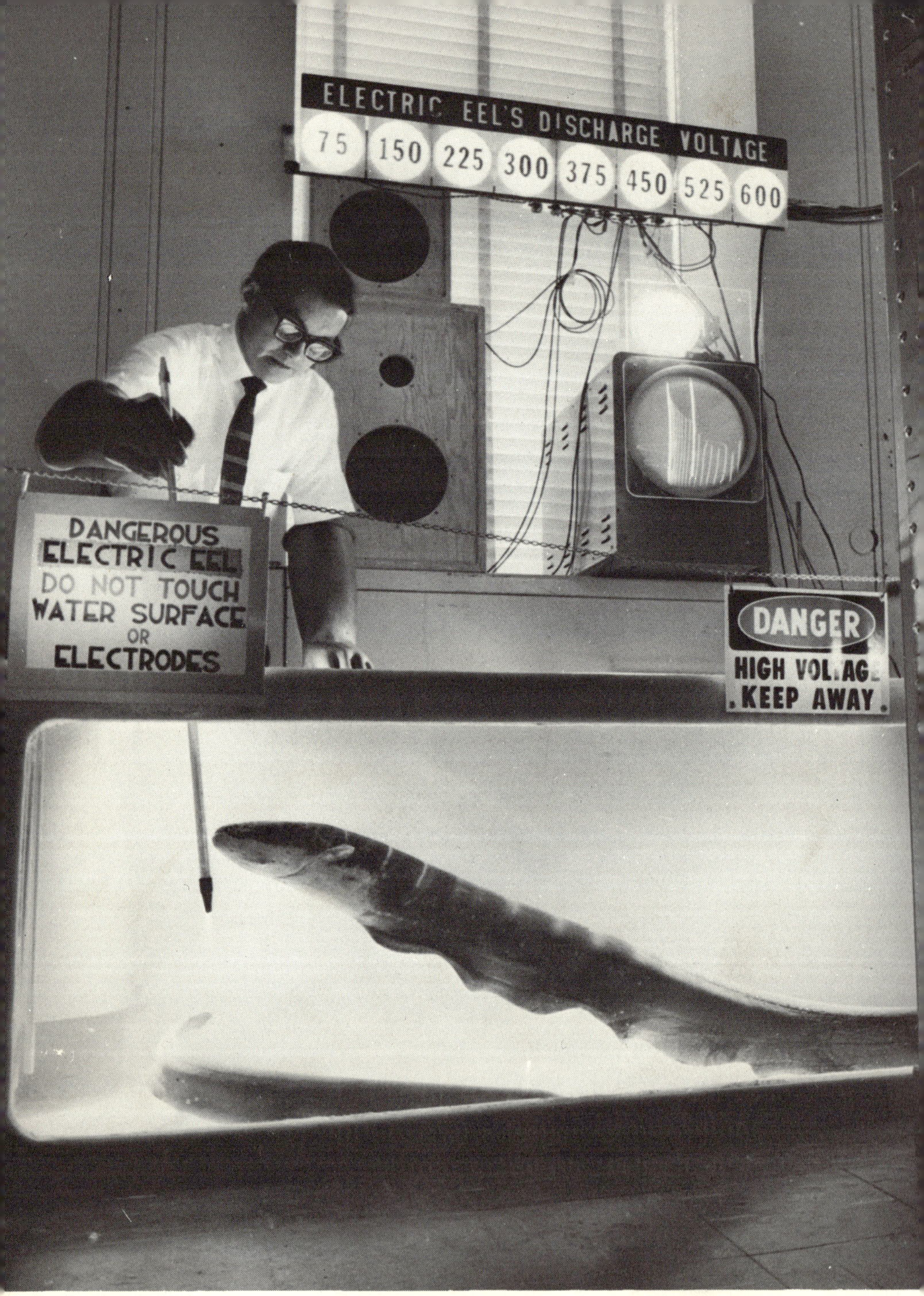

Electric eels can be as dangerous as high voltage wires. This one generates 600 volts, enough to kill a man.

nerve cells of an eel. While this cell lived in a nutrient solution, he carefully implanted tiny electrodes at each end. With oscilloscopes and electronic amplifiers he studied how impulses flashed through these cells.

The instruments showed that each cell kicked out one-tenth of a volt as long as it remained healthy. But when he added chemicals related to the deadly nerve gas to the nutrient solution, the cell's electric generating capability petered out like an old flashlight battery.

Dr. Nachmansohn began probing into how these deadly chemicals did their work. Slowly, through tedious work that involved long hours of chemical analysis, he discovered how the eel's cells generated electricity and how these signals were blocked.

Dr. Nachmansohn's work was all the more complex since one of the biochemicals responsible for nerve impulses existed for only fractions of a second. A stimulus to a nerve, Dr. Nachmansohn proved, produced a biochemical called acetylcholine. This biochemical allows an electric impulse to stream through nerve fibers. But if acetylcholine remains in a nerve, another, unwanted, effect occurs. The nerve keeps on relaying electric charges that generate at random, causing dozens of haphazard electrical signals to flow through the nerve. More important, these signals prevent other, vital signals from being transmitted. And, when a nerve's electrical circuitry is swamped with incoherent, random signals an animal soon dies.

Nature prevents this from happening by wiping out acetylcholine with another biochemical. With the thick, plentiful nerve cells of the electric eel as a research tool, Dr. Nachmansohn showed that after a signal passed through a nerve, an enzyme called cholinesterase neutralizes the acetylcholine. And, with acetylcholine out of the picture, the nerve is ready for a new signal. The time needed for cholinesterase to erase acetylcholine from a nerve cell is measured in millionths of a second.

And nerve gases? They inactivate cholinesterase. And, with this substance out of action, acetylcholine remains in the nerve fibers. Quantities of random impulses flash through the body's circuits. Muscles begin to twitch, at first gently, then violently. The affected animal goes into uncontrollable spasms. Muscles stop functioning and the victim can't breathe. Soon it dies.

Dr. Nachmansohn, and another researcher who joined his team, Dr. Irwin Wilson, used up many more barrels of electric eels to find these facts. But, once known, work on an antidote began.

The idea for this lifesaving drug was simple. Design a chemical that would combine with the nerve gas and render it harmless. After further months of arduous work, Dr. Wilson created a compound that chemically combines with nerve gas, rendering it inactive. Cholinesterase resumes its job of neutralizing acetylcholine. With acetylcholine gone, random nerve pulses stop cluttering up the body's circuitry, and important messages begin to flow freely again. Once this chain of chemical events is over, an animal's spasms disappear. It begins breathing normally. And, of course, it lives.

The German government never used the nerve gases it developed. In fact, Dr. Wilson perfected the antidote after the war ended. But soon, what was an antidote for nerve gas found another use.

After World War II the same chemicals composing nerve gas were adapted to pesticides. Instead of killing men, the gases, chemically turned into powders and liquids, killed insects.

It didn't take long before carelessness and misuse of insecticides caused accidental poisoning and deaths among agricultural workers. Japan, a country that uses vast quantities of these insecticides on its rice fields, had an especially high rate of agricultural deaths due to insecticides.

Suddenly, research on the electric eel had a new significance. The antidote developed for poison gas wasn't needed. But that same drug would also cure poisoning by insecticides. Today, this drug, commonly called PAM, is credited with saving the lives of over 5,000 agricultural workers in Japan alone.

Now, PAM is stocked around the country, ready for quick distribution to areas where insecticide poisoning crops up. When the city of Tijuana had its epidemic, emergency supplies were rushed there from a nearby storage area, undoubtedly saving dozens of lives.

Meanwhile, in aquariums throughout the country a favorite display is that of an electric eel in a long tank. Two or three times a day, a worker wearing thick rubber gloves touches the eel. Lights around the tank flash on from the electricity the eel generates while children squeal and shout in amazement.

Perhaps only a few people who've seen such a display realize that the same nerves feeding electricity to the lamps were important research tools leading to the development of a drug that has already saved thousands of lives—and will almost certainly cure many more thousands of people poisoned by insecticides.

CHAPTER SIX

Mice to Clams to Drug

Sometimes it's a chance observation by a marine scientist that leads to a biochemical that might someday serve man. More often, a researcher's long, tedious hours of analyzing and testing uncovers a potential drug from Davy Jones's locker.

Then, there are the accidents, when someone stumbles across a vastly important biochemical completely by chance. This is how the clam, one of the best known and tastiest of marine creatures, became the focus of interest for one researcher. From an unexpected and puzzling fact this scientist discovered about clams has come a biochemical, now being tested in the laboratory, that shows remarkable potential as an anticancer drug.

This biochemical might not yet have been discovered if laboratory mice weren't so expensive.

Mice might be pests to homeowners. But they are a necessity to biological researchers. These animals are easy to keep and handle. More important, strains of mice have been bred to have certain characteristics. One strain, for example, has a tendency to become infected with tumors. Another strain was bred to be tumor resistant. With identical strains of mice available, research teams throughout the country can test the same drug, or conduct the same experiment, knowing that each mouse in a given strain reacts the same as all others.

But laboratory mice cost about 75 cents each. And, with laboratories sometimes using dozens a day, mice put a sizable dent in a research budget. At least that's what Sister Arline Schmeer, a Dominican nun, thought while she was working at the Marine Biological Laboratory (MBL), Woods Hole, Massachusetts.

Sister Schmeer had been interested in cancer research years before coming to the MBL. At Ohio Dominican College she had tested various anticancer drugs on mice, and later, at Sloan Kettering Memorial Institute in New York, she tested these drugs on cells growing in nutrient solution. When she arrived at the MBL, Sister Schmeer's project was to find a cheaper laboratory animal in which cancer cells could be implanted, grown, then tested with new anticancer drugs. A common sea animal, she thought, would be perfect. There are plenty of them, they're easy to gather, and in tanks of seawater, almost as easy to keep as mice.

Shellfish—abalones, clams, oysters, barnacles, for examples—were one group of sea life Sister Schmeer considered as possible research animals. But almost immediately she ran into a perplexing snag. After reading dozens of scientific papers written over the last decades about shellfish, Sister Schmeer noticed that there was not one reported case of any of these creatures getting cancer.

Marine animals are just as prone as land animals to diseases like cancer, tumors, viral infections, abscesses, and other maladies. Shellfish, like their fellow sea creatures, should have had an incidence of cancer. All the more so since some shellfish, clams for instance, live to be 40 and 50 years old. So many clams living to that age without any sign of cancer was not only a curious observation, it was an extraordinary fact.

Naturally Sister Schmeer checked her findings with fellow researchers at the MBL. None had ever heard of or seen a case of cancer in shellfish. But many insisted that this was just a coincidence, and began looking through still more scientific papers and research notes. Despite this thorough probing, not one case of shellfish cancer turned up. A fact available for years had finally been stumbled over and noticed.

Sister Schmeer abandoned her project of finding a cheap experimental laboratory animal. Instead, she began searching for the reason shellfish appear immune to one of man's most common diseases.

The first step was to learn if shellfish could transfer their resistance to cancer to land animals. Sister Schmeer removed the shells from many different kinds of shellfish and ground up the soft insides of each variety. Next, in a centrifuge, she separated the liquid part from the solid. Then she injected the raw liquid into mice that had cancer.

After months of experimentation with different shellfish she learned that many kinds of these animals retard cancer in mice. One species stood out: the common cherrystone clams, eaten by the thousands each year, contained the most lethal biochemical to cancer cells; it was harmless to normal cells. She named this biochemical mercenene, from the scientific name of the cherrystone or quahog clam: *Mercenaria, mercenaria.* Without even being chemically identified, this anticancer biochemical had its name.

About this time, Sister Schmeer left the MBL and returned to Ohio Dominican College. There, she started the traditional—and laborious—work of isolating the single biochemical responsible for retarding cancer in mice.

First, the clams, minus their shell, were ground up in a special blender. This mixture, which looks like a chocolate milkshake, is then put in a centrifuge. Any solid matter settles to the bottom of the container, leaving a brown liquid, the raw extract, on top.

Then, she isolated the various biochemicals in this brew. One standard laboratory technique used was column chromatography. A glass tube about two feet long was filled with a special powder; the size of each powder grain being exactly the same. Then the raw clam extract, or any other liquid with several unknown biochemicals, was poured in the top. The powder acts as a sort of molecular sieve. The biochemicals that have the smallest molecules flow into the powder and are trapped. Those with the largest, heavier molecules flow through the powder to a lower level. The biochemicals of about the same molecular size finally settle at specific heights in the column of powder. Scientists call each layer of biochemicals in the powder a "fraction."

Next, each fraction was washed from the powder and tested for its anticancer action. The fraction or fractions that showed the biological activity being studied were purified even further.

Using column chromatography, Sister Schmeer found that raw clam extract divided into 32 fractions. Over a period of several years, she tested each fraction on mice infected with cancer, finally isolating the single fraction that saved the lives of animals with this disease, and determining the smallest dosage that yielded results.

The amount of mercenene necessary was miniscule. Sister Schmeer injected about as much as can fit on a match head—eight thousandths of one gram—into cancer-ridden mice for seven days. Another group of mice, called a control group, and also infected with cancer, received injections of salt water. After ten days or so the control group died. At least 80 percent of the other group—the ones receiving mercenene—lived, and bred normally. Their children were normal too, a sign that their parents had been cured of the malignant cell growth.

Six months later, long after the mice ordinarily would have been dead, Sister Schmeer dissected the animals. Scar tissue dotted the areas where the tumors had begun to grow before mercenene was injected. The cancer cells did make headway at first, but then were stopped and killed by this biochemical.

No scientific discovery is considered valid unless qualified researchers can duplicate the results. Soon after Sister Schmeer's discovery of mercenene, Nobel prize winner Albert Szent-Gyorgyi, who met Sister Schmeer at the MBL at Woods Hole where he had been conducting research of his own, confirmed her observations. The effects of mercenene were no fluke.

Still another scientist, Dr. C. P. Li, a world-renowned scientist then working at the National Institute of Health near Washington, D.C., decided to see for himself if mercenene is an anti-cancer drug, or if simply some accident or other unexplained circumstance had produced Sister Schmeer's results.

Dr. Li was familiar with sea animals as he was also experimenting with shellfish, including the conch, sea snail, and the abalone. Dr. Li had found that extracts from many shellfish are deadly to certain kinds of bacteria. Then, he and his research team found that another factor in shellfish extracts acted against viruses, including those that cause polio and influenza.

These discoveries, which are still being investigated as other potential marine drugs, are equally important because drugs acting against viruses are rare. There is still no drug that counters the common cold, for example. So any hint of a possible antiviral drug, from marine animals or elsewhere, is a major find. Dr. Li called the active agent against bacteria Paolin I—paolin being the Chinese word for abalone.

This common and edible soft-shell clam produces a possible anticancer drug. Extracts from other shellfish have acted against viruses, including those that cause polio and influenza.

Paolin II is the agent which acts against viruses.

Since many scientists now believe that a connection exists between virus and cancer, it was natural for Dr. Li, immensely interested in the antiviral activity of shellfish extracts, to see if Sister Schmeer's mercenene was really a cancer inhibitor. He used much the same process of extracting the biochemical from clams, and then tested it on hamsters infected with cancer. He confirmed the basic observations of Sister Schmeer.

Well before mercenene approaches the realm of a full fledged drug, Sister Schmeer has to solve some mysteries surrounding the biochemical. For one: mercenene from one batch of clams sometimes results in a 100 percent cure when injected into cancerous mice. Mercenene extracted from clams from a different part of the sea bed and at a different time of year might only cure 75 percent of infected mice.

Also, this biochemical seems more effective when extracted from clams during the summer, when sea water is warmer than during winter months. Just why temperature—if this is the reason—affects a clam's production of mercenene is another item to be resolved.

But the biggest problem confronting Sister Schmeer and the research team she heads is identifying the exact molecule that does the job of inhibiting and retarding cancer cells. Sister Schmeer and other researchers analyzing mercenene know that it's a rather small molecule. But still, they haven't yet pinned down its exact chemical formula. Until this is done the drug can't be artificially duplicated in laboratories. So, all the mercenene available today comes from clams. Consequently, there isn't enough of the biochemical to answer still one more vitally important question: Does mercenene work on spontaneous tumors?

Many drugs will cure artificially implanted tumors in mice and other laboratory animals. But these same drugs don't always cure tumors that develop naturally in animals and people. Some preliminary but isolated experiments indicate that mercenene does inhibit malignant tumors that grow spontaneously in humans. But Sister Schmeer cautiously warns that until mercenene is available in larger quantities these results can't really be tested further and confirmed. And, until clinical experimentation is terminated, mercenene stays classified as an experimental drug.

Right now, much research time, effort, and money are directed at pinning down the formula of the elusive biochemical that clams so easily manufacture. But even before mercenene's chemical composition is known, and then synthesized in laboratories, the lowly clam has joined the list of marine animals that have contributed a potentially vital drug to man's weaponry against disease.

CHAPTER SEVEN

Deadly Fish of the Deep

The marine researcher, looking for samples of a rare fish, swam lazily underwater, his snorkel sticking up from the sea's surface like a periscope. Scanning the sandy bottom 18 feet or so below, he spotted a weever fish half buried in a sand bank. He dove, and with a heavily gloved hand reached for the animal. At first, the weever swam idly away from the outstretched hand. Then it struck.

With a burst of fury, the fish sped upward, twisted, and faced the diver, its fins vibrating ominously. After a moment's pause it raced toward the man and brushed his jaw with the stiff, needle-sharp spines on its back.

The diver swam toward shore 500 feet away, the puncture bleeding slightly. But within a minute a venom injected by the fish's spines began its work. A slight sting felt in the jaw turned quickly into enveloping pain. Soon the man's entire head and chest throbbed with pile driver force. He found it hard to raise his hands for the next faltering strokes, and slowly sank.

Friends came to his rescue. By the time he was dragged up on shore his body had begun to swell. Razor-sharp pain sped throughout his body, and later he described breathing and swallowing something akin to "...being engulfed in liquid fire." By the time he reached a hospital, his body had blown up almost beyond recognition. No pain killer helped the bursting agony and the man begged to be killed.

For days the weever fish's venom acted on his victim's body. The man's skin became bluish. A massive blood clot formed on his face, and blood vessels broke inside his skin. Only after many days of this hell did the symptoms begin to subside. Weeks later, when he left the hospital, his skin was still off-color, his face slightly swollen. The only reason he lived was because the weever fish had only brushed his face, failing to deliver a lethal injection of poison. There is no antidote for a full dose of this—and most other—marine venoms.

The poison released by the weever fish is simply one of several toxic substances produced by fish, many of which cause paralysis, hallucinations, and death. But these fish toxins, harmful and often deadly in pure form, represent important therapeutic resources of the sea. Right now, many fish poisons that kill or maim are being investigated in laboratories for their possible use as beneficial drugs.

For instance, puffer fish found in warm water oceans, blow up like balloons when faced with danger. Their fantastic increase in size, plus prickly spines on their bodies, make them hard

In prescribed doses, the deadly venom of the puffer fish is widely used as a pain killer in Japan, but formal testing of the drug is still going on in the United States.

to swallow—an effective protection against predators.

At least 40 species of puffer fish also manufacture one of the most potent poisons known to man. This deadly biochemical is concentrated in the interior organs of the fish. In Japan, where puffers are considered a prime delicacy, these entrails are removed before the fish is cooked.

Yet, even a scrap of a puffer's organs can cause death, and cases of puffer fish poisoning and consequent fatalities abound in Japan. Today, only specially trained chefs, licensed by the Japanese government, are allowed to prepare puffer fish. These chefs are trained at special schools to remove all traces of the poison-laden organ.

The fact that puffers manufacture a powerful poison didn't escape notice of Japanese doctors. They saw that this toxic substance caused progressive numbness, a tingling sensation in the hands and feet that gradually grasps the entire body. Soon, loss of feeling, total numbness, and inability of muscles to carry out normal tasks such as breathing, result in death for the victim.

Over 100 years ago, a Japanese doctor, despite primitive laboratory methods then available, isolated the biochemical responsible for this toxic action. He called the substance tetrodotoxin. From duplicating his methods, today's researchers know that this doctor's preparation was so impure it held only a small fraction of tetrodotoxin. Still, in controlled doses, the drug gained widespread importance as a pain killer throughout Japan.

Today, tetrodotoxin, in pure form, is widely prescribed in Japan to ease the sledgehammer throbs of migraine headaches, to relax muscle cramps, and as a general pain killer. In the United States, tetrodotoxin hasn't yet gained recognition as a legitimate drug since the years of testing needed to gain formal approval from governmental agencies hasn't been carried out.

Still, one other reason tetrodotoxin isn't yet

found on drugstore shelves is that researchers are faced with an unusual problem. Marine pharmacology is such a new field that scientists are quite often occupied with isolating the exact chemical structure of biochemicals found in sea plants and animals. This isn't the case with tetrodotoxin. Chemists have found the molecular structure of the drug. But they haven't carried this discovery one step further: pinpointing the exact *part* of the molecule that does the job.

Chemists know that a single section of a molecule can be responsible for a biological effect, and that another section can cause an unwanted side reaction. So, they often try and strip a molecule of the part they suspect causes toxicity, or unwanted effects. So far, tetrodotoxin hasn't yielded to this chemical plastic surgery. Consequently the drug has unpleasant side effects that do not meet pharmaceutical standards in the United States. When the section of the molecule causing these side effects is discovered and chemically removed, tetrodotoxin might well gain acceptance as a new and potent, non-addictive pain killer.

Besides the puffer, other fish are contributing strange and powerful biochemicals to the list of possible drugs. A toxin produced by one fish—its exact name is held confidential for reasons covered later, but it is often called the "dream" fish—might someday be useful in treating mental illness.

South Sea natives have long known that the flesh of some fish causes hallucinations. Intrigued by these reports, scientists at the World Life

Research Center in California, an organization investigating pharmaceutical potentials of marine life, gathered some of these animals. From the "dream" fish they isolated what they suspected was a mind-manipulating drug. To find out its exact effects, the research team drew lots. The winner was given a small dose of the substance. A few minutes later the man became haunted by a fear of impending death. Sweat broke out on his face and his hands trembled as the sensation of dying increased. Soon, he became convinced that he was dead, and lay down on a cot in total stupor. This conviction lasted 12 hours or so. By then, the worst effects had worn off. Later, the researcher described this period as ". . . enough to make the worst nightmare seem like a picnic."

The drug's effects persisted. After 24 hours, the deep depression and yet persisting conviction of death disappeared. But the man remained a will-less robot, blindly following the orders of others without question, a state that lasted for days.

To what good this biochemical can be put remains the province of further research. But those investigating this and similar marine drugs hope they can be used as a tool to help pry open the mysteries of the mind, and perhaps even as a new treatment for certain mental disorders.

The fact that these marine mind drugs might have military applications hasn't escaped notice. If dropped on an army such a mind drug could turn troops into robots, mentally incapable of any action. This is partly why the exact name of this fish that sent a researcher into believing his own death is held a closely guarded secret.

Other fish are just as virulent, but in a different way. The stonefish habitually burrows into sand on the sea's bottom. It looks like a brownish, mottled stone benevolently waiting for a scuba diver to pick it up.

Any that do court death.

The stonefish, for all its quiet demeanor, sports spines on its back that deliver one of the most painful and deadly venoms known. When touched, stonefish swirl up in aggressive fury and attack what they consider an enemy. Spines erect, they flash toward the intruder, spin, and stab the needle pointed spines in their victim.

The puncture wounds are deceptively tiny, about as large as those a needle would make. Intense, sharp, sometimes burning pain follows immediately. Within three to five minutes the pain spreads from the puncture site. Victims of stonefish stings report that the agony becomes uncontrollable. Many of those stung thrash about violently. Those who are lucky lose consciousness.

But the worst comes an hour or so later. Delirium, lowered body temperature, and severe headaches occur in the days and weeks following. The skin, even far removed from the site of the sting, becomes inflamed and painful when touched. Swelling begins, and soon the entire body anywhere near the punctures becomes practically unrecognizable because of its bloated size. Limbs nearest the sting often become paralyzed.

The stonefish appears to be a harmless rock on the sea floor, but the spines on its back deliver one of the most painful and deadly poisons known.

Death usually follows within six hours. But there are cases on record where symptoms persisted for six months, killing the victim after this time. If the person lives, the sensation of numbness in limbs near the sting can last for years afterward. Sometimes this partial paralysis never leaves the victim.

The venom of this fish hasn't yet been tamed for use as a drug. But researchers at the School of Medicine of the University of Southern California did look into the biological effects of the venom in controlled experiments. These scientists noted that one fraction of the poison—a single biochemical isolated from the many in the venom—reduced the coagulation time for blood, and drastically lowered blood pressure of experimental animals. Other fractions caused death. With more time and money available for research, this powerful poison might be honed into a new and valuable anticoagulant, as well as a drug that reduces blood pressure.

The poison of the weever fish might also lead to a new pharmaceutical. At the laboratory of Neurological Research of the College of Medical Evangelists in Los Angeles, marine researchers found that injections of weever fish venom caused profound changes in the action of the heart, blood vessels, and respiration. Shortly after injection, the pulse rate of experimental animals slowed dramatically. Blood pressure fell, and respiration became more widely spaced. Eventually the animal died. Not a good sign of a potential drug, except the venom did produce effects surgeons could use for patients undergoing certain operations: slow heartbeat and lowered blood pressure.

These experiments used pure weever fish venom. With the active biochemicals isolated, and the toxic biochemicals scrapped, this fish poison, like many others that have never even been tested for biological effects, might someday be turned into commonly used drugs.

CHAPTER EIGHT

A Bloom of Red

There's no predicting when it will happen. One day the sea is a normal pale green or blue. The next morning the color includes a faint tinge of red-brown. Day by day this tint of rust grows darker and spreads further, until it covers dozens of square miles of water—as far as the eye can see. This growth is the red tide.

Red tides are due to a fantastic growth spurt of phytoplankton, single-celled marine organisms generally classified as plants. During the morning hours the sea's surface is densely packed with these free-floating plant cells. Then, as the sun rises higher in the sky, the cells slowly sink lower in the sea. By mid afternoon, most are yards below the ocean's surface and the reddish tinge becomes fainter.

The color resumes its full hue during the morning hours as the plants again swarm toward the sea's surface. A single quart of water scooped up at this time holds 10 to 30 million of these plant cells.

Besides reacting to strong sunlight by sinking, a bloom of red tide phosphoresces during the night. If the ocean is disturbed by a ship or an oar, the roiled water softly glows with an eerie beauty. Red tides have an additional, important characteristic: they produce a toxin that is more powerful than strychnine.

For natives living off the sea, the time of a red tide is a period of fear and extreme caution. Shellfish such as clams and mussels become deadly to eat. Many fish also become poisonous—if they are able to live at all. During one intense bloom of red tide off the coast of Florida, thousands of fish died in the first few days. By the time the bloom had disappeared—as quickly and mysteriously as it had begun—it had killed over 200 million pounds of fish.

Marine scientists believe that red tides coincide with a sudden wealth of nutrients that upwell from ocean currents, or that are washed into the sea from rivers. The exact nutrients necessary, as well as other conditions that foster red tides are still a mystery.

It was while looking into this puzzle of a red tide's sudden growth that a marine scientist found its potential usefulness. The same deadly poison that kills fish, and sometimes men, contains a strong antibiotic.

Discovery of the red tide's antibiotic agents was practically an accident. "I was studying the biology of Phosphorescent Bay off Puerto Rico and came across a bloom of red tide," explains Dr. Paul Burkholder, among the country's foremost marine researchers. "I wondered if the poison was antibiotic and looked into it more out

Effects of the red tide: tons of dead fish. This one-celled organism blooms without much warning, turning the sea a rusty brown color and killing most marine life that come in contact with it.

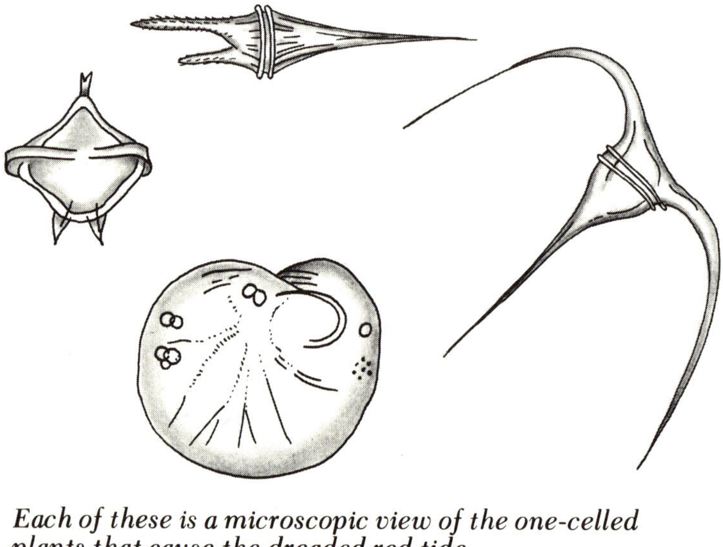

Each of these is a microscopic view of the one-celled plants that cause the dreaded red tide.

of scientific curiosity than anything else."

To collect the red tide's plant cells Dr. Burkholder bought fifteen large plastic garbage pails. He and his crew filled the pails with seawater full of the plants. Then, they covered the pails with blue cellophane, which simulated the sky during late afternoon. The cells sank to the bottom of the pails, just as they sank below seawater when the sun was low in the sky.

After an hour or so the crew poured off the water and collected the thin film of rust-colored sludge on the pails' bottoms. About 3,000 gallons of water, and several days later, Dr. Burkholder had collected about one pound of the single-celled plants.

To separate the plant cells from bits of organic matter in the sludge, Dr. Burkholder strained the gooey mass through a fine filter. He made thick cakes of the plant cells, froze some to prevent decaying, and made immediate tests with the others.

Preliminary experiments proved that these plants, now removed from seawater, were still deadly. Small fish put in jars holding the dried plants died within minutes. Once having shown that the poison was still active, Dr. Burkholder tested it against a wide variety of harmful germs and other growths. He streaked the plant cells across colonies of germs, yeasts, and varieties of harmful fungi living in nutrients. Within a day the results were obvious.

The species of plant cells that caused the red tide in Puerto Rico's Phosphorescent Bay killed penicillin-resistant staph germs, a variety of other microbes, and a pathogenic yeast that causes serious infections in the mouth and other mucous membranes of humans.

This discovery caused a flurry of excitement among the research team. Of all the drugs available today none can be guaranteed to wipe out staph infections. Still fewer are completely effective against the particular yeast that the red tide wiped out. If the particular biochemical or biochemicals that did these jobs could be isolated, Dr. Burkholder and his team might have in hand a particularly valuable group of new drugs.

Typically, singling out the potentially helpful biochemicals from the dozens of others in the red tide's toxin was a laborious and time-consuming job. Dr. Burkholder brought back cakes of the red tide he had frozen to Lamont Geological Observatory in New York. At the Marine Research Laboratory at Lamont, he isolated the red tide's active elements—finally deriving a bit of powder that barely covered the bottom of a thimble. After testing and preliminary analysis of the powder, he and his research associates had a surprise. The red tide actually produced *three* distinct antibiotics, each with different characteristics.

The results of Dr. Burkholder's work have been published in scientific journals, and since that time he has gone on to experimental work with sponges. The three possibly useful antibiotics are awaiting the years of further testing and research needed for all therapeutic contenders to reach drugstore shelves. But, like so many other promising drugs from the sea, lack of money, researchers, and facilities block more extensive experimentation. When the facilities and money are found, it will be up to other marine researchers to continue perfecting the red tide's toxin into useful drugs.

But one pharmaceutical originating from a sea plant doesn't need further research. Paradoxically, this biochemical is derived from among the largest sea plants, a brown seaweed known as giant kelp.

Giant kelp grows in huge ocean beds in shore waters off the Pacific coast. These kelp beds vary in size, and typically are anywhere from a few hundred feet to a mile wide and several miles long. Besides being one of the largest marine plants, this kelp is among the fastest growing. A single plant, with large flat leaves attached to a long stalk by a bulbous stem, can grow one to two feet in a single day.

Preferably, giant kelp grows in water 25 to 80 feet deep, where it can cling to rocks on the ocean bottom. Strong currents renew the huge quantity of nutrients the kelp needs to sustain its rapid growth.

As early as 1883 scientists found that giant kelp, and other varieties of brown seaweed, contain a useful industrial chemical called algin. Recently researchers have discovered that sodium alginate, a variety of the industrial algin, is a drug that can eliminate radioactive strontium 90 from the body.

Gleaning the raw algin from giant kelp and other brown seaweeds is a straightforward, industrial process. First, giant harvest ships run through the kelp beds automatically snipping off this seaweed about three feet below the water's

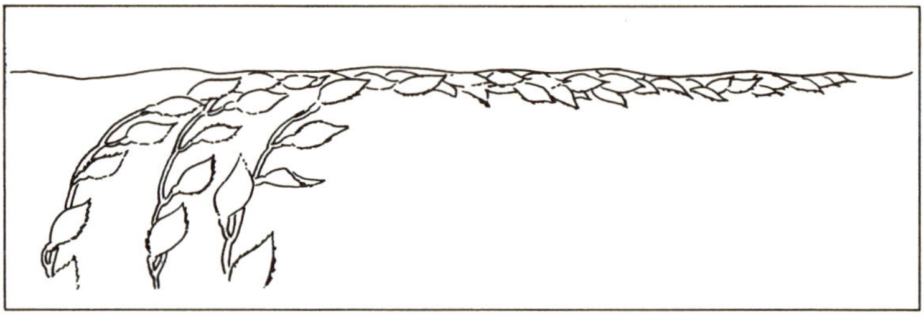

Giant kelp grows in ocean beds from a few hundred feet to a mile wide and several miles long. These plants, which are harvested commercially by huge ships, are the basis of an antiradiation drug.

surface. As the ship slowly plows its way through the beds, a tramway lifts the harvest into a huge bin. When the bin is full, the ship heads for its dock, where the day's catch of kelp is unloaded. Since the harvest ship only cuts off the top of the plant, the kelp remains healthy and soon grows new leaves.

At the shore-side kelp factory, the plant is processed to extract the algin much as it was in the 1800's, including washing, filtration, pressing, rinsing, and several other well-known manufacturing steps. The final product is a white powder.

Dr. D. Waldron Edward, an English biochemist, became interested in this white powder during World War II, when she was working in England. During this war, the English population's diet sadly lacked vital minerals. Dr. Waldron experimented with using brown kelp and its by-product, algin, as a source of these minerals. Her experiments failed. For some reason the human body simply eliminated the algin without absorbing the sodium, calcium, and other minerals it contained.

Later, Dr. Edward came to Canada and started work on a different problem—how to inactivate radioactive strontium 90 from the body.

One of the by-products of an atomic explosion is radioactive strontium 90, a mineral very similar to calcium. The two minerals are so alike, in fact, that the body can't distinguish between them. Radioactive strontium 90 is absorbed and used to build bones, or replace bone cells, as readily as its mineral cousin calcium. But the radioactivity of this strontium produces deadly results, including cancers and destruction of bone cells.

Spread by an atomic explosion, strontium 90 eventually falls over large areas, including croplands, pastures, and water supplies. If people eat the crops, drink the water or milk from cows eating pastureland infected with strontium 90, the mineral eventually ends up in their bones.

Dr. Edward and her colleagues, including Dr. Stanley Skornys and Dr. T. M. Paul, were looking for a way to purge deadly strontium 90 from living bone. Many of their early experiments would have done more harm than good. Once in the bone, the radioactive mineral can only be removed by leaching out almost all minerals—a process that leaves the bones little more than rubbery cartilage. Obviously this procedure would be disastrous.

Then, Dr. Edward remembered her wartime experiments with algin. She wondered if this biochemical might somehow eliminate strontium 90 from a person's intestines before it was absorbed by the body.

Over several years, the research team, working at Canada's McGill University, experimented with the derivative of algin called sodium alginate. They fed this biochemical to rats, who also ate food contaminated with radioactive strontium. When the rats' bones were later tested, the research team found little of the radioactive substance. Yet, the bones contained the normal amount of calcium.

Sodium alginate, the research team found, somehow bound itself chemically with the mineral strontium, but didn't bind itself to the calcium. The rat eliminated the sodium alginate, along with most of the radioactive strontium, but digested the calcium.

Medical ethics and common sense prevent these experiments, where radioactive materials are swallowed by the subjects, from being carried out on human beings. But they have been tested on other animals. And, all evidence indicates that sodium alginate will operate as well on humans as on experimental animals. So, if an accidental explosion at a nuclear power plant, or other atomic accident, takes place, there is a drug available that will protect the populace from radioactive strontium, one of the most feared and deadly side effects of atomic explosions.

The red tide and brown sea kelp are only two among a handful of ocean plants that are being exploited today. The sea contains hundreds of other marine plants, and undoubtedly a wealth of pharmaceutical and therapeutic agents are growing there for the taking.

CHAPTER NINE

The Odds and Ends of the Sea

It was a balmy, cloudless day in 1945 when Dr. Giuseppe Brotzu, an Italian biologist, waded into the warm waters off the coast of Sardinia. He was taking no pleasure in the sea this day. Instead of wandering over bright sand-filled beaches of this Italian-owned island, he chose to walk in the waters where the sewer systems of Cagliari, Sardinia's largest town, emptied into the oceans.

Dr. Brotzu chose this spot on a hunch. As an official of Cagliari's Institute of Hygiene, he was concerned with outbreaks of intestinal ills that periodically swept the island's population. These outbreaks—a menace to public health—could be controlled with public health measures. But, Dr. Brotzu was hoping to find a specific drug that would act against the bacteria causing infections and upsets of the digestive system.

These harmful bacteria, obviously, would occur in great numbers at the sewer outlets of the city. And, Dr. Brotzu guessed, these outlets were also a logical place to look for natural enemies of these same bacteria. Perhaps some, he thought, could be transformed into a useful pharmaceutical against the disease-causing microorganisms.

At first, Dr. Brotzu collected various kinds of bacteria and seaweeds, testing them against the harmful germs. He found none that were effective. Then, one day, he scraped a bit of fungus from a rock near a sewer outlet, sealed it in a collection bottle, and brought it, along with other items he gathered, to his laboratory.

There, he ran customary tests with his day's harvest. Most items had little or no effect on the harmful bacteria. The fungus did. Bits of this living matter wiped out entire colonies of deadly germs living in nutrients, including those that caused the intestinal disturbances common to the island.

For three years Dr. Brotzu studied this fungus, with astounding results. For one thing, it wasn't toxic. Even huge amounts of the growth, when injected into mice and other laboratory animals, didn't cause death or other serious side effects. Then, in addition to acting against germs causing intestinal diseases, it killed a wide variety of other deadly microbes.

Finally, Dr. Brotzu tested this fungus on humans. He grew colonies of it in a nutrient and made a fluid extract. He injected this extract into patients who were seriously ill with the dreaded staphylococci and streptococci microbes, as well as the germs causing typhoid fever, undulant fever, and brucellosis. Most patients improved dramatically: many were cured. And, as Dr. Brotzu was quick to point out, the active biochemical in the fluid extract was in an impure and weak form.

At this time Dr. Brotzu had none of the advanced laboratory equipment necessary to isolate and analyze the single active biochemical in the fungus that killed these microbes. He published the promising results of his work in an Italian scientific journal. Then, for lack of equipment, he stopped further research.

By a fluke, a British health officer ran across Dr. Brotzu's article. He notified some researchers in England about the fungus's action, and scientists there took up the research where Dr. Brotzu had left off. For years, the English team grew different strains of the fungus, isolated the active biochemicals, and analyzed them. One important characteristic of the fungus's antibiotic spurred them on.

Many disease germs by this time had become immune to widely used antibiotics, notably penicillin. Some strains, staphylococci, for instance, had evolved an enzyme that destroyed penicillin, and hence were immune to the drug. But the antibiotic from Dr. Brotzu's fungus was powerful enough to kill many of the same microbes that could shrug off even massive doses of penicillin.

Because of this fact interest in the fungus's antibiotic spread, and researchers in the United States also began perfecting what they thought was a promising new drug. Through a process called molecular manipulation, biologists actually altered the antibiotic's chemical structure in different ways, attempting to build a drug that acted against an even wider variety of microbes while having little or no side effects on people.

Finally, in 1964, 19 years after Dr. Brotzu first discovered the antibiotic, such a drug was tailored from the fungus's basic antibiotic biochemical. Today, it is manufactured synthetically in large quantities by the Eli Lilly Company, and distributed under the name Keflin and Keflex. It is used as a broad spectrum antibiotic, and is often effective where penicillin and other "wonder" drugs simply don't work at all.

The years of research needed to perfect a usable drug from a bit of fungus demonstrates how the odds and ends of the sea can, ultimately, be wrenched into service for mankind. Today, many researchers are on the trail of a promising substance from marine life that may or may not be eventually harnessed to man's service. Among the many examples: the barnacle.

Barnacles begin life as tiny eggs, then free-floating larva that bear no resemblance to the final animal. Like many insects, they undergo periodic molts, changing form seven times, taking about one day for each stage. Before their last and final change, they find something solid to stick to—a pier, ship's hull, rock, etc. Then, through tiny antennae, the barnacle secretes a rubbery glue. Within 15 minutes this glue has hardened, fastening the barnacle to its perch for life. Crude laboratory tests show that for every square inch of surface stuck with the barnacle's glue, a force of 22 pounds is needed to yank the bond apart. Constant exposure to sea water, changing temperature, and swift ocean currents don't affect this cement. It is one of the most stable, durable, and permanent adhesives made by nature.

Barnacles secrete one of the most stable, durable, and permanent adhesives made by nature. Scientists are hoping it can be used to stick fractured bones together or to bind new teeth to bone.

The starfish has the amazing ability to regenerate itself, as can be seen by this baby starfish growing from the severed arm of an adult. Perhaps someday, the biochemicals responsible for this might be used to stimulate the growth of new limbs in human amputees.

And, it is one of great interest to the medical profession. Surgeons could use a strong glue that sticks fractured bones together while they knit and mend. Dentists are hopeful that barnacle glue can be used to bind new teeth to bone, or hold caps on a ground-down tooth.

So far, the raw glue taken from barnacles seems resistant to the enzymes in the mouth and those naturally occurring in the body—giving strong promise it can be used in humans. Right now, researchers are still attempting to pin down the chemical nature of the barnacle cement so it can be manufactured in large quantities. If and when they do—and if the glue lives up to its early promise—the barnacle will be added to the long list of marine creatures that satisfies man's medical needs.

Among the most fascinating areas researchers are probing are the bizarre and often mysterious physical properties shown by marine life. These alien and even grotesque capabilities of many marine organisms probably hold the secrets to many of the fundamental processes of life.

The starfish is a good illustration.

Cut an arm off a starfish and it grows another. More significant, the arm sprouts nerves and muscle and becomes another starfish. This process, scientists think, is controlled by special hormones and enzymes secreted by the starfish's cells. But what are these hormones and enzymes, and how do they stimulate production of a new starfish?

Long-range research into this creature's rejuvenation powers could well lead to the discovery of biochemicals that might restore damaged nerves in human beings. One other hope—admittedly long-range—offered by the starfish: that the biochemicals responsible for their rejuvenation powers might also be used to stimulate growth of new limbs, fingers, or toes of amputees.

Strange? No more so really than an anticancer drug from clams, an antibiotic from red tide, or a heart stimulant from a hagfish.

Even stranger, perhaps, is the bizarre hormone produced by a sea worm called Bonellia. This foot-long worm, found in warm water seas, produces larvae that swim close to the mother worm before taking off on their own. Any larvae that touch the mother's body become male worms. These cease growing and live a parasitic existence inside another female. The larvae that fall to the sea floor without having touched the mother worm become females.

A powerful water-soluble hormone makes the difference. The female worm secretes this hormone from her body wall and a mouthlike snout at her head. Experiments to date show that this hormone, in various dilutions, can induce different degrees of masculine or female characteristics in Bonellia worms.

The same hormone also halts development of sea urchin eggs. More, when the eggs of a sea urchin are dosed with a weak solution of the Bonellia worm's hormone, they sink to the bottom of their tank and begin to disintegrate. Within an hour they simply disappear.

Just what biochemical in this hormone possesses the power to inhibit growth remains to be discovered. When isolated it certainly will be put

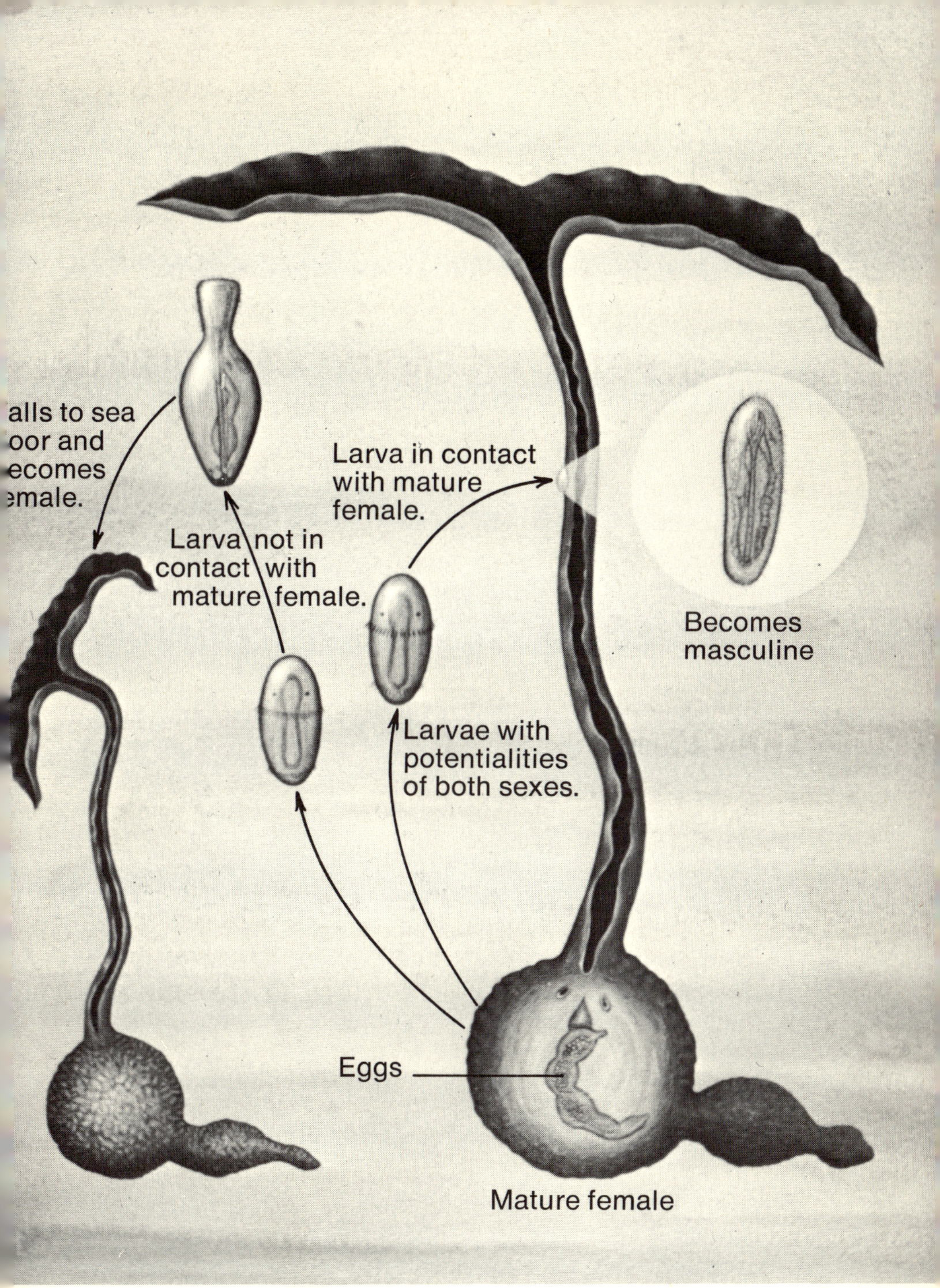

A powerful hormone secreted by the mother Bonellia worm causes any of her offspring which touch her snout to stop growing and become male. The others fall to the ocean floor and develop into females.

to use in experiments where growth inhibition is important. Among these, of course, is with cancer cells grown in a test tube.

The jellyfish is still another marine creature offering a contribution to medical science. During the night jellyfish often glow with a soft eerie intensity. Scientists at Princeton University and at the University of California found that when a particular biochemical manufactured by jellyfish contacts calcium in the animal's body, this biochemical emits light. They isolated the substance and called it aequorin. The more calcium aequorin touches, the brighter it glows.

Now, aequorin is being put to vital use in measuring the quantity of calcium in blood and muscles. Doctors have long known that calcium has something to do with muscle contraction. But they don't know exactly where in the muscle the element acts, how much is needed for contraction in all cases, and the amount, if any, used up at each contraction.

With aequorin as a measuring tool they are finding out. Researchers now spread a tiny bit of this biochemical over contracting muscle cells. Wherever aequorin contacts calcium, it releases a tiny flash of light. Special cameras record the intensity and location of these flashes. Later, when reviewing the film, scientists can accurately measure how much calcium the cells used, where it was used, and how fast it was depleted.

With the help of the jellyfish biochemical, physiologists are now pinning down the role of calcium in heart contractions, experiments that

A jellyfish glowing in the dark. The substance that produces this light is now being used by doctors to measure calcium levels in blood and muscles.

could lead to more effective treatment of many kinds of heart disease.

The same technique can determine the amount of blood calcium, important for clotting. A dilute solution of aequorin is mixed with blood and slipped under delicate instruments that measure even the dimmest light. The brightness with which the aequorin glows accurately indicates the amount of calcium in the blood. Before scientists found this biochemical in the jellyfish, they had no effective and rapid way to measure blood calcium.

Are there other examples of ocean life aiding man?

Sure, and more appear every year as marine scientists continue probing the mysteries of the deep. Even so, the fantastic variety of life forms living in the vastness of earth's waters hold medical secrets that scientists can now only dream about. Given that only a small fraction of our seas' organisms have so far been explored, Davy Jones's locker remains a pharmaceutical cornucopia that has just barely been tapped.

Index

A Note About The Author

James R. Berry has been a science writer for the last fifteen years. His numerous articles have appeared in such magazines as *Today's Health*, *Science Digest*, *Today*, *Popular Science*, and many others. He has also written many film scripts, and recently wrote and produced a film dealing with heroin addiction for the National Institute of Mental Health. Mr. Berry has also written several books for children and young adults. He lives in Brooklyn, New York, with his wife, who is a science teacher, and their three children.